TAKE CONTROL OF YOUR MIND AND DOMINATE YOUR LIFE: THE MINDT MANUAL IS YOUR SECRET WEAPON!

Raffaele Vertaglia

"The best way to get started is to stop talking and start doing." - W. Disney

INTRODUCTION

Mindt is an innovative methodology based on the use of mind mapping and visual thinking techniques to improve information management and creativity. This introductory course has been designed to provide a comprehensive overview of the main techniques and tools used in Mindt, in order to allow participants to acquire the necessary skills to apply these methodologies in their daily work.
The course is structured in a practical and easy-to-follow way, with a series of exercises and activities that allow participants to directly experience the learned techniques. During the course, you will cover topics such as mind mapping, information management, data visualization and problem solving.

The course is aimed at professionals from all sectors who wish to improve their productivity and creativity, but also at students and enthusiasts who wish to deepen their knowledge in this field. No specific previous knowledge is required, just curiosity and desire to learn.

By the end of the course, participants will be able to create effective mind maps, handle information more efficiently, and develop new ideas more creatively. Furthermore, they will have acquired a greater awareness of their own cognitive abilities and will have learned to make the most of them.

In conclusion, this introductory course at Mindt is a unique opportunity to acquire innovative and useful skills for your work or study. Thanks to its practical and easy-to-follow structure, it is suitable for all those who want to improve their productivity and creativity.

Take control of your mind and dominate your life: The Mindt Manual is your secret weapon!

Mindt's Handbook

by Raffaele Vertaglia

Translate by GOOGLE

Are you tired of feeling helpless, like your mind is out of control? Do you feel that your emotions, your fears and your thoughts are conditioning and limiting you in everyday life? It's time to take control and dominate your life!
And the Mindt Handbook is your secret weapon for doing just that.
Imagine waking up every morning with a mental clarity that allows you to face any challenge with confidence and determination. Think how wonderful it would be to free yourself from the shackles of irrational fears, bad thoughts and limiting beliefs that drag you down. The Mindt Handbook is your travel companion in this extraordinary adventure towards mental transformation.
Through pages filled with wisdom and knowledge, you'll discover the secrets to unlocking your mind's limitless potential. You will learn to recognize and overcome the obstacles that keep you from achieving the happiness and success you deserve. With practical exercises, guided meditations and proven strategies, the Mindt manual will lead you towards a deep awareness of yourself and your inner power.

It's not just about acquiring theoretical knowledge. The Mindt Handbook will guide you step by step, day after day, in the practical application of what you learn. Through the power of positive habits, you'll learn to reprogram your mind for success. You will see tangible changes in your life as you practice the techniques and strategies shared in the manual.
But Mindt goes further. It is an invitation to transform your entire existence. You will discover how to cultivate healthy and fulfilling relationships, how to manifest abundance and prosperity, how to find your true purpose in life. The mind is the starting point for anything you wish to achieve, and Mindt gives you the keys to unlocking the doors of infinite opportunity.
Don't let your mind be your invisible enemy. Regain your rightful power and live a life filled with joy, success, and fulfillment. The Mindt Handbook offers you the opportunity to radically transform the way you think, feel and act.
Every page of this manual exudes passion, compassion and empathy. The best techniques and

strategies from the most advanced disciplines in the field of human potential have been brought together. Experts in psychology, neuroscience and spirituality have come together to create a one-of-a-kind work that will guide you on your journey of personal growth.

The Mindt Handbook is an investment in yourself, your happiness, and your success.

It is an opportunity to awaken your dormant potential and reveal your true essence. Don't postpone your future anymore. Take control of your mind and start mastering your life today. The Mindt Handbook will support you every step of the way, because you deserve to live the extraordinary life you've always dreamed of.

CHAPTER 1. DEFINITION OF MINDT AND ITS BENEFITS: DISCOVER A NEW DIMENSION OF INNER WELL-BEING.

Welcome to the fascinating world of Mindt, a journey of awareness that will guide you towards a more serene and fulfilling life. Mindt, an acronym for Mindfulness Training, is much more than just a practice: it's a key that will allow you to unlock the hidden treasures within yourself.

Imagine living each day without the stress and anxiety that often overwhelm us. Mindt offers you this possibility, reducing stress and bringing a sense of calm and tranquility into your life. Thanks to your new awareness of the present moment, you will be able to face daily challenges with a clear and clear mind.

Mindt is also a gift to your mind. Regular practice will allow you to increase your concentration, strengthen your memory and develop greater self-awareness. You will be able to live every moment in a more intense and profound way, fully appreciating the wonders that surround you.

But the benefits don't end there. Mindt teaches you to manage your emotions in a healthy and balanced way. You will no longer be a slave to your impulsive reactions, but will gain the ability to respond thoughtfully and compassionately. Mindt will help you cultivate a harmonious relationship with yourself and others by improving your social interactions and relationships.

Mindt is also good for the soul. With it, you will learn to embrace the present moment with gratitude and acceptance. You will not let the past imprison you or the future worry you. You will live in the here and now, savoring every moment as a precious gift.

To fully experience Mindt's benefits, it's important to make time for it every day. Even just a few minutes of regular practice can make a difference. Find a quiet place, away from distractions, and immerse yourself in this practice that will transform your life.

I warn you: Mindt requires commitment and perseverance. But the journey you embark on will be filled with startling discoveries and profound transformations. Every day, you will move towards a new dimension of inner well-being, where you will find the peace you have always longed for.

Don't wait any longer! Embrace Mindt and begin your journey to serenity and authentic joy. Get ready to open the doors to a wonderful world and discover all that your mind and heart can offer. Mindt awaits you with open arms.

CHAPTER 2. THE FUNDAMENTAL PRINCIPLES OF MINDT.

In this lesson, we will delve into the fundamental principles of Mindt, a working methodology that focuses on optimizing cognitive performance and maximizing mental efficiency.

The first fundamental principle of Mindt is mindfulness. It consists of being aware of your thoughts, emotions and actions at all times. This allows us to better manage our cognitive resources and avoid losing mental energy in useless or distracting activities.

The second fundamental principle is concentration. It consists of being able to focus on important tasks and ignore distractions. Concentration is a critical skill for success in any field and can be developed through mental training.

The third fundamental principle is creativity. It consists of being able to generate new ideas and innovative solutions to problems. Creativity can be stimulated through exploring new ideas, observing the world around us and using specific techniques.

The fourth fundamental principle is memory. It consists of being able to memorize important information and to recall it when necessary. Memory can be improved through the use of specific techniques, such as mnemonic association and repetition.

The fifth fundamental principle is communication. It consists of being able to communicate effectively with others, both verbally and non-verbally. Effective communication is a critical skill for success in any field and can be developed through mental training.

Finally, the sixth core principle is stress management. It consists of being able to manage stress and anxiety effectively in order to maintain optimal mental and physical balance. Stress management can be improved through the use of specific techniques, such as meditation and deep breathing.

In summary, the core principles of Mindt are mindfulness, concentration, creativity, memory, communication, and stress management. These principles are essential for optimizing cognitive performance and maximizing mental efficiency, and can be developed through mental training and the use of specific techniques.

CHAPTER 3. HOW TO USE MINDT IN YOUR WORK.

The Mindt is a very useful tool for those who work in various sectors, as it allows you to organize your ideas and structure your work effectively and efficiently. To make the most of Mindt in your work, it is important to understand its features and learn how to use them comprehensively.

First, it is essential to create a detailed mind map, which includes all the information necessary for the work at hand. The mind map must be organized in a clear and logical way, in order to facilitate the understanding of the information and their management.

A mind map is a graphical representation of the ideas, concepts and connections that form in our minds. It's a powerful tool that helps us organize and display information in a clear and intuitive way. Drawing up a mind map is a creative and liberating process, which allows us to express our ideas and explore new paths of thought.

To draw up a mind map, follow these steps:

1. Start with a central theme: Write the main theme of your mind map in the center of the sheet or blackboard. It can be a keyword, concept or image that represents the main topic.

2. Add main branches: From the central word, draw lines or arrows branching outward. On each line, write a word or short phrase that represents an idea related to the main theme. These words or phrases will be your main branches.

3. Add Sub-Branches: Each major branch can be further developed with sub-branches. Draw lines or arrows from main branches and write words or phrases on them that represent more specific or detailed concepts.

4. Use colors and images: You can make your mind map more lively and inspiring by using different colors for words and branches. You can also add images or symbols that visually represent ideas or concepts.

5. Create Connections: Connect branches and sub-branches that are related to each other. You can use lines, arrows, or simple curves to show conceptual connections.

6. Be flexible and creative: There are no hard and fast rules in creating a mind map. Be open to experimentation and let your creativity flow freely. If a new idea or link pops into your head in the process, add it to your mind map.

The mind map is a dynamic and constantly evolving tool. You can add, edit or delete information according to your needs. It's a versatile tool that can be used for taking notes, organizing ideas, planning projects, or studying.

Creating a mind map allows you to visualize the relationships between ideas intuitively and to have an overview of the topic being discussed. It helps you spark your creativity, organize information logically, and generate new connections and thought associations.

Experience the magic of mind maps and discover how they can broaden your thinking capacity, improve your memory and spark your creativity. Be free to explore, to play with ideas and to let your mind open to new horizons. Mind maps are your ally on the journey of discovery and exploration of your inner world and the knowledge that surrounds you.

Once you've created your mind map, you can use it as a guide for getting the job done. For example, if it is a research project, the mind map can be used to organize the information gathered and to define the phases of the work to be carried out.

Also, the Mindt can be used for time management. For example, you can divide your work into several phases and define a deadline for each phase. This way, you can monitor the progress of your work and make sure you meet deadlines.

Imagine that you are holding a detailed mind map in your hands, a compass that guides you through the sea of information. Mindt offers you this valuable tool, which will allow you to organize your ideas in a clear and logical way, simplifying your work and improving your productivity.

When you create your mind map, immerse yourself in a world of creativity and intuition. Let your mind flow, free and expand, connecting ideas in a natural and flowing way. The resulting organization will surprise you: each piece of information will find its place and will harmoniously connect to the others, creating a complete and well-structured picture.

Think for example of a research project. Your mind map will be the beacon that lights the way. You will be able to enter all the collected information, sources, key concepts and salient points. Each branch of the map will lead you to a new discovery, a new piece of the puzzle you are assembling. The Mindt will allow you to keep track of the phases of the work, dividing the project into clear and achievable stages.

But Mindt doesn't stop there. She also helps you manage time, a precious commodity that often gets out of hand. Using your mind map as a guide, you can divide the work into different phases and assign a deadline to each one. This will allow you to constantly monitor your progress and make sure you meet the deadlines you set for yourself. You will be the captain of your ship, leading your project to the port of success.

Let the Mindt turn into concrete action. Each branch of your mind map will be a road you will travel, a goal you will reach. Your productivity will increase, your mind will feel light and you will enjoy a sense of accomplishment that will fill you with joy.

Don't miss your chance to turn chaos into order, free yourself from clutter and live your life more efficiently and fulfillingly. Mindt is your secret ally, ready to give you the clarity and structure you need to bring your projects to life. Embrace her and let her accompany you on this extraordinary adventure.

Finally, Mindt can also be used for team management. For example, you can create a shared mind map with all team members to facilitate communication and collaboration. In this way, each team member can view the information in a clear and organized way and contribute to the achievement of common objectives.

In conclusion, the Mindt is a very useful tool for those who work in different sectors and can be used exhaustively to organize one's ideas, manage time and the team. To make the most of it, it is important to understand its features and learn how to use them effectively and efficiently.

CHAPTER 4. MINDT'S TECHNIQUES FOR PROBLEM SOLVING.

Lesson 4 is devoted to Mindt's techniques for comprehensive problem solving. This approach is based on the use of a structured method for analyzing and solving problems, which consists of five stages: problem definition, problem analysis, solution development, selection of the best solution, and solution implementation.

The first stage, problem definition, is to identify the problem and define it clearly and precisely. It is important to understand the context in which the problem occurs, its effects and causes, in order to be able to analyze it effectively.

The second phase, the analysis of the problem, involves the identification of possible solutions. In this phase we try to understand the reasons for the problem and identify the options available to solve it. It is important to consider all possible alternatives, even the less obvious ones.

The third stage, solution development, is the generation of ideas to solve the problem. In this phase, innovative and creative solutions are sought, which can be implemented effectively and sustainably.

The fourth stage, the selection of the best solution, involves evaluating the different options and choosing the most suitable solution. It is important to consider the advantages and disadvantages of each option, as well as weigh the long-term costs and benefits.

Finally, the fifth phase, the implementation of the solution, involves applying the chosen solution and monitoring the results obtained. It is important to verify that the solution works correctly and produces the expected results.

Mindt's techniques are useful for solving complex problems and dealing with difficult situations effectively. This approach allows you to systematically analyze problems and identify the best solutions, ensuring greater effectiveness and greater efficiency in problem solving.

When we are faced with complex problems and difficult situations, Mindt proves to be a powerful weapon to deal with them successfully. This practice offers you a systematic approach that allows you to analyze problems in detail, identifying the most effective solutions and paving the way for success.

Imagine having a beacon in the storm, a compass that guides you through the challenges life presents you. Mindt offers you this beacon, this compass, which will allow you to navigate confidently even in the roughest waters. By approaching problems with an approach based on mindfulness and emotion management, you will be able to maintain the mental clarity necessary to find the best solutions.

Mindt teaches you to observe problems without getting overwhelmed by the negative emotions they can generate. You will be able to analyze the situation objectively, breaking down the problem into small elements and identifying hidden connections. In this way, you will have a clear and complete vision of the picture, allowing you to evaluate possible solutions with lucidity and intuition.

But Mindt goes beyond analysis: it also gives you the tools to take action. Thanks to your focused mind and awareness of the present moment, you will be able to develop concrete strategies and implement them effectively. You will face challenges with determination and courage, overcoming obstacles one after another.

Mindt allows you to be more efficient in solving problems. With a systemic and aware approach, you will avoid getting lost in irrelevant details or making hasty decisions. Your mind will be a powerful ally, able to analyze the options, consider the consequences and choose the best path.

Don't let problems get you down. Choose to face them with Mindt, a practice that will give you the power to solve the most complex situations successfully. Recognize your potential and make the most of your mental abilities. Mindt is here to guide you to victory, enabling you to overcome every obstacle and achieve the happiness and success you deserve. Trust it and experience the transformative power it can bring into your life.

CHAPTER 5. HOW TO USE MINDT TO MAKE DECISIONS.

Mindt is a methodology that can be used to make decisions comprehensively. It involves analyzing all aspects of the problem to be solved, evaluating the different options available and choosing the best solution on the basis of objective criteria.

To use the Mindt you need to follow some basic steps. First, it is necessary to clearly define the problem to be solved, identifying the objectives to be achieved and the limitations to be considered. Secondly, all possible solutions to the problem must be identified, weighing their pros and cons and comparing them with each other.

Once the available options have been identified, we move on to the phase of selecting the best solution. In this case, it is important to base yourself on objective and quantifiable criteria, such as cost, time needed to implement the solution, impact on available resources, and so on.

To use Mindt successfully, follow these basic steps that will lead you to troubleshooting in an effective and exciting way.

Start by clearly identifying the problem you want to solve. Make a mind map of your challenges, goals to achieve, and limitations you need to consider. This initial phase will allow you to have a clear and complete vision of the situation, paving the way for your creative mind.

Next, let your mind go free, exploring all possible solutions to the problem. Imagine that you have a color palette in front of you and you paint the options one by one. Evaluate the pros and cons of each solution, allowing room for your intuition and inner wisdom.

Once you have a range of solutions in front of you, it's time to select the best one. Rely on objective and quantifiable criteria, such as cost, time required to implement the solution, impact on available resources, and so on. See beyond the emotions of the moment and make informed decisions that will bring you closer to your goals.

Using the Mindt in this process allows you to bring awareness and presence into your decision making. Observe your emotions as you explore your options and consider your state of mind when making your choice. Be kind to yourself and rely on the intuition that comes from your Mindt practice.

Remember that there is no perfect solution, but rather a solution that best fits your specific needs and circumstances. Mindt offers you the key to unlocking the creative potential that resides within you and to making decisions that will lead you to your happiness and success.

Face your problems with confidence and serenity, knowing that you have the tools to find the brightest solutions. Mindt is your faithful ally, ready to guide you along the way. Be open to exploration, experiment boldly, and enjoy the problem-solving process. Success awaits you, and Mindt will guide you to a life full of extraordinary achievements.

Your choices are like brushstrokes on a vibrant canvas of possibilities. Mindt offers you a space of creativity and connection with yourself that allows you to make decisions with an open heart.

Remember that you are more than just a problem to solve. You are a unique human being, with dreams, passions and desires guiding your path. Mindt invites you to consider these aspirations as you consider solutions, because your happiness is central to solving the problem.

Take a deep breath and let Mindt envelop you like a gentle caress. Carry love and compassion with you as you move through the options, knowing you are doing your best. Remember that while there is no perfect solution, you have the ability to make wise choices that are respectful of your values.

Mindt connects you with your inner wisdom, with that voice that guides you to the path of truth. Listen carefully as you consider solutions, feeling your intuition playing like a melody in your heart. Let your soul express itself through your choices, creating a unique harmony in your path.

Don't be afraid of making a wrong choice. At Mindt, every choice is an opportunity for growth and learning. Embrace the process and welcome challenges as opportunities to evolve and discover sides of yourself that you didn't know.

And when you finally arrive at the solution that resonates most authentically with you, celebrate it as a personal victory. Feel proud that you have walked this path with awareness and care. You trusted Mindt and found a way to a solution that makes you vibrate with joy.

The Mindt is a trusted companion who accompanies you in solving problems, in creating your destiny. Trust it, immerse yourself in the flow of awareness and let your mind and heart come together in a harmonious dance. Your life is an ever-creating masterpiece, and with Mindt, the picture you paint will be extraordinary.

Finally, it is important to monitor the implementation of the chosen solution, verifying that it produces the expected results and promptly intervening if not. In this way, it can be ensured that the decision made is really effective and that it produces the desired results in the long term.

In summary, the Mindt is an effective methodology for making decisions in an exhaustive manner, based on objective criteria and evaluating all the possible options available. By following the fundamental steps of Mindt, it is possible to find the best solution to the problem to be solved and guarantee the success of the action taken.

CHAPTER 6. MINDT'S ROLE IN STRESS MANAGEMENT.

Mindt, an acronym for Mindfulness Training, is a technique that is becoming more and more popular as a tool for stress management. It is based on mindful attention to the present moment, without judgment and with acceptance.

Mindt, the enchanting Mindfulness Training, is a precious gift that is increasingly gaining ground as a stress management tool. It is a safe haven in which to find peace and serenity, and will lead you towards a more aware and fulfilling life.

Imagine immersing yourself in the present, feeling every breath, every sound, every sensation that surrounds you. Mindt invites you to do so, to let go of past and future worries, and immerse yourself completely in the here and now. It is a balm for the soul, which allows you to turn off the noise of the mind and connect with the deep inner stillness.

With Mindt, you will discover the art of paying attention with love and kindness. You will learn to listen to your body, to recognize the tensions that build up and to release them with the power of conscious breathing. You will notice the thoughts floating in your mind, but you will not get attached to them. You will observe them like clouds passing in the sky, letting them go gently.

Mindt will teach you to bring attention to the present in every aspect of your life. When you walk, you will feel the contact of your feet with the ground, the air caressing your skin. During meals, you will savor every bite, appreciating the flavors and textures like a precious gift. You will be present in your relationships, listening to others with genuine attention and responding with love and compassion.

This practice is not limited only to moments of calm and meditation. You can also apply Mindt during daily activities. Imagine carefully washing the dishes, feeling the water flowing through your hands, perceiving the softness of the soap and the brilliance of the ceramic. Observe how this simple action transforms into an act of gratitude and presence.

Mindt offers you a safe haven in which to find comfort when stress takes its toll. With her power, you will be able to face life's challenges with greater equanimity. You will recognize the emotions that arise in your heart, welcoming them with kindness and understanding that they are part of the human experience. You will no longer be a prisoner of stress, but will become the master of your mind.

Experience the miracle of Mindt, immerse yourself in this wonderful practice and you will discover the hidden treasure in the present moment. Your breath will become the melody of your life, awareness will guide you towards inner balance. Trust it, because it will lead you to deep peace and lasting well-being.

Mindt is like a tender hug that envelops you when you are overwhelmed by stress. It's a haven of calm and tranquility where you can find relief and recharge. Mindt's practice gives you powerful tools to manage stress in healthy and effective ways.

Imagine feeling the tension melt away in your body as you practice Mindt. Your shoulders relax, your breathing becomes deep and rhythmic. With each inhalation, feel the stress drift away, while with each exhalation you let go of the worries and tensions that have built up. In this space of presence and acceptance, you discover that you are stronger than you think and that you can face life's challenges with courage.

Mindt invites you to become aware of your thoughts, without judging them or identifying with them. Observe your thoughts as clouds floating in the sky, without letting their power carry you away. With constant practice, you will develop a calmer and more resilient mind, capable of facing challenges in a balanced way.

But Mindt goes beyond stress management. It opens doors for you to discover a depth of connection with yourself and the world around you. You connect with the beauty of small moments, like the sound of rain beating on the roof, the scent of flowers wafting through the air or the sweetness of a sincere hug. Mindt reminds you to appreciate these daily gifts and to live with gratitude.

Mindt is not only an individual practice, but can also be shared with others. You can create a Mindt space with family, friends or in a professional setting. Sharing moments of presence and deep listening with the people you care about creates authentic connections and strengthens ties. Together, you can support each other on the path to well-being and happiness.

Mindt is a beacon of light in the storm of daily stress. It invites you to slow down, reappropriate the present moment and take care of yourself. No matter how intense the world around you, Mindt reminds you that you have the power to cultivate inner calm and find peace in your life.

With Mindt, you give yourself the gift of well-being and serenity. Be kind to yourself and remember that practice takes time and perseverance. Face challenges with compassion and determination, knowing that you have Mindt as a reliable ally along the way.

Experience the wonder of Mindt and discover the immense power of this practice in managing stress and living a fuller and more authentic life. Trust Mindt and let her gentleness and wisdom accompany you on your journey of transformation.
To understand Mindt's role in stress management, it is necessary to consider that stress is a physiological response of our body to situations perceived as threatening or dangerous. When we are subjected to excessive and prolonged stress over time, our body can suffer physical and psychological damage.

Mindt can help manage stress in several ways. Firstly, it allows you to develop greater awareness of your emotions and thoughts, allowing you to identify situations that generate stress and act on them more effectively.

Additionally, Mindt's can help reduce emotional reactivity, or the tendency to overreact to stressful situations. Indeed, thanks to Mindt's practice, one learns to observe one's emotions without judgment and not to let oneself be overwhelmed by them.

Mindt can also help improve the quality of sleep, reduce anxiety and depression and increase resilience, or the ability to face difficulties and overcome them.

To get the benefits of Mindt it is necessary to practice it regularly. The practice can take place in different ways: through meditation, conscious breathing, observation of one's thoughts and emotions. To fully immerse yourself in the benefits of Mindt, it is essential to set aside regular time for the practice. This transformational journey can take place in many ways, through practical methods that allow you to discover the salient points of this extraordinary discipline.

Meditation is one of the fundamental pillars of the Mindt. Find a quiet place, sit comfortably, and start directing your attention to your breath. Notice the movement of the breath going in and out of your body, without trying to change it. With patience and kindness, let your mind relax, letting go of passing thoughts. Be present in the moment, without judging, welcoming whatever arises into your awareness.

Mindful breathing is another powerful technique for connecting with the present. Bring your attention to your breath, observing it as a guide that reconnects you to the present moment. As you inhale, feel the vital energy entering your body. As you exhale, let go of tensions and worries. Take a few moments to consciously breathe throughout your day, reminding yourself to return to your breath as anchors of calmness and presence.

Observation of thoughts and emotions is a crucial aspect of Mindt. Be a neutral observer of your mind, recognizing the thoughts that arise and letting them flow without identifying with them. Observe the emotions that arise, welcoming them with kindness and understanding. Remember that you are neither your emotions nor your thoughts, but an aware observer who can choose how to respond.

Beyond the specific techniques, Mindt also develops in your everyday life. Bring awareness into your life, pay attention to the activities you carry out, without haste or distraction. Savor the food you eat, enjoy contact with nature, listen to others with genuine attention. Every moment can become an opportunity to practice Mindt and embrace the beauty of the present.

Remember, however, that Mindt requires practice and consistency. Start with small steps, dedicating a few minutes a day to your practice. Over time, you will be able to gradually extend the duration and intensity of your practice, enjoying its ever more profound benefits.
Explore Mindt's various practices, finding the ones that resonate with you the most. Let Mindt become a natural reflection in your life, a habit that supports you on your path to mindfulness and well-being.

Mindt is a treasure that you can discover and cultivate every day. Be open to experience and let your practice develop with love and patience. Through regular Mindt practice, you will open the door to a new level of awareness, peace and joy that will accompany you on your life journey.

In conclusion, Mindt represents an effective tool for stress management, which can be used by anyone who wants to improve their quality of life. Thanks to the practice of Mindt it is possible to develop greater awareness of one's body and mind, reduce anxiety and emotional reactivity and increase resilience.

CHAPTER 7. HOW TO USE MINDT TO ENHANCE CREATIVITY.

Mindt, an acronym for "Mental Imagery and New Directions in Thinking", is a technique that can be used to enhance creativity. It is based on the use of mental images to generate new ideas and solutions. In this way, Mindt can be useful in different contexts, such as in solving problems, strategic planning and generating new ideas for products or services.

Mindt, the incredible "Mental Imagery and New Directions in Thinking", is a powerful ally to unlock your creativity and allow your ideas to dance with freedom. With Mindt, you can open the doors of your imagination and discover new horizons of innovative thinking.

Imagine immersing yourself in a world of vivid and inspiring images that reside in your mind. Mindt invites you to create detailed mental images, to visualize scenarios, objects or people that can stimulate your creativity. You can explore fantastic landscapes, paint pictures with your mind, or imagine new perspectives for solving problems that come your way.

Mindt finds application in many contexts. For example, if you are struggling with a complex problem to solve, you can use your creativity to imagine different possible solutions. Mentally visualize each option and let your mind explore the details and implications of each choice. You may surprise yourself by discovering innovative ideas that you would never have considered otherwise.

In the context of strategic planning, Mindt can be a valuable guide. Imagine creating a visual mind map of your plan, with each branch representing a possible direction. Visualize the results you want, imagine the steps needed to achieve them, and let your creativity guide your mind along bold new paths.

As part of generating new ideas for products or services, Mindt can be an inexhaustible source of inspiration. Close your eyes and imagine the product or service you want to create. View the details, features and benefits it offers. Let your mind wander into uncharted territories and be amazed by the insights and ideas that emerge.

Mindt invites you to embrace the beauty of imagination and experience the power of mental imagery. There are no limits to your creativity when you open the doors of your mind and allow ideas to flow freely. Mindt gives you the wings to fly into the infinite dimension of your imagination, bringing with it the promise of new horizons, innovative solutions and a world of possibilities.

Trust Mindt and discover the transformative power of mental images. Be inspired by the magic of your creativity and let your ideas shine like bright stars in the firmament of your mind. Mindt accompanies you on your journey to creation, offering you an exciting experience of exploration and innovation.

When you embrace Mindt and let mental images dance in your mind, you discover a world of emotion and inspiration that urge you to explore your creative potential. It's a fascinating journey, where your ideas come to life and become tangible realities.

Imagine immersing yourself in a vivid and immersive mental image. You can feel the texture of objects, perceive the vibrant colors that surround them, savor the scents floating in the air. Every detail comes to life, becomes real in your imaginary world. It is in this space of creativity that the most daring and innovative ideas are born.

The Mindt allows you to range beyond the boundaries of tangible reality, to embrace the unknown and to explore new dimensions of thought. You can immerse yourself in fantastic worlds, invent incredible characters or imagine enthralling scenarios. Your mind is free to experiment, to push boundaries, and to make surprising connections between ideas.

On your journey of creative exploration, Mindt offers you a reliable compass. You can use mental imagery to generate new perspectives and innovative solutions to problems you encounter along the way. These images will guide you in new directions, allowing you to overcome obstacles with a spirit of innovation and daring.

Mindt also teaches you the importance of trusting yourself and connecting with your emotions. As you immerse your mind in the images, pay attention to any emotions that arise. Be aware of how these emotions affect your creativity and welcome them kindly. Mindt invites you to let your emotions fuel your creative process, adding a touch of authenticity and depth to your ideas.

Use Mindt to generate new ideas for your work, your personal projects or your life in general. Mentally visualize your goal, immersing yourself in the details and vision of the results you want to achieve. Let your mind free itself from restrictions, exploring new avenues and making unexpected connections.

The Mindt is the portal that allows you to access a world of creative potential that resides within you. Rely on his loving guidance and experience the joy and excitement that arise from your creativity. Discover the thrill of turning your ideas into concrete reality and sharing your creative gift with the world.

Remember that you are a born creator, full of resources and potential. With Mindt as an ally, you can push the limits of imagination and create extraordinary works. Experience the magic of mental imagery, embrace your creativity and let your ideas take flight. Mindt supports you every step of your creative journey, illuminating the path with light and inspiration.

To use Mindt to its fullest, it is important to follow a few basic steps. First, it is necessary to identify the problem or the goal to be achieved. Once this is done, you can proceed to the "guided imagination" phase, during which you try to visualize the solution to the problem or the innovative idea you want to develop.

Mindt is like a vivid and emotional painting, a work of art that manifests itself through your creativity. With it, you can explore the boundaries of your imagination, break the shackles of the ordinary and immerse yourself in extraordinary worlds.

When you give yourself the gift of Mindt, you discover a universe of emotions that intertwine with your ideas. You can feel the passion burning in your chest as the images unfold in your mind. Enthusiasm vibrates in your hands, ready to bring your boldest visions to life.

Mindt invites you to experience the power of imagination in every aspect of your life. You can use it to explore new perspectives, to turn difficult situations into opportunities and to create beauty from every experience. Your creativity becomes a beacon that lights the way and opens doors to new horizons.

Imagine using Mindt to solve complex problems. Mentally visualize the challenge you are facing and let your creativity flow. Observe how the images take shape and connect to each other, generating innovative and surprising solutions. Mindt guides you beyond limitations, allowing you to find unexpected ways to success.

In the fields of planning and innovation, Mindt can be your most trusted ally. Imagine creating a mind map of your ideas, where each image represents a step towards your goal. This visual journey allows you to explore the connections between ideas, to discover new directions and to outline a winning strategy. Mindt teaches you that there are no limits to your creativity and that your potential is unlimited.

The Mindt can also be a portal to beauty and inspiration. Imagine immersing yourself in a mental image that evokes deep emotions, which awakens your senses and ignites your passion. These images can turn into works of art, touching writings or projects that bring light into the world. Mindt invites you to give your creativity to the world, to share your unique gift and to inspire others with your vision.

Trust Mindt and let your mental images become a source of inspiration and creative power. Feed your creativity the care and love it deserves. Don't be afraid to explore uncharted territory and embrace your uniqueness. Mindt supports you in your artistic research and pushes you to give shape to your wildest dreams.
Experience the wonder of Mindt and discover the immense beauty that resides in your creativity. Let the images dance in your mind, transforming themselves into masterpieces that testify to your essence. With Mindt as your guide, you will become an artist of life, painting your world in vibrant colors and conveying deep emotion with every brushstroke of your creativity.
During this phase, it is important to let your imagination run free and not limit yourself to already known or pre-packaged solutions. Techniques such as metaphor or analogy can also be used to stimulate creativity and generate new ideas.
Once the possible solutions or ideas have been identified, it is important to critically evaluate them and choose the one that best suits the context in which one operates. In this sense, Mindt can also be useful for evaluating different options and choosing the best one.
In conclusion, Mindt can be a very useful technique to enhance creativity and generate new ideas and solutions. To use it exhaustively, it is important to follow some basic steps, such as the identification of the problem or the goal to be achieved, the guided imagination phase and the critical evaluation of the possible solutions.

CHAPTER 8. HOW TO DEVELOP AWARENESS IN THE MINDT, METHODS AND PRACTICAL TRICKS.

Awareness is a fundamental quality for psychological and physical well-being. In the Mindt, mindfulness is a key element in achieving inner peace and improving the quality of life. There are several methods and practical tricks to develop awareness in the Mindt.

Mindfulness is a precious gem in Mindt's treasury. It is the beacon that illuminates the path to inner peace and well-being. Through the practice of Mindt, you can develop mindfulness in surprising and profound ways, allowing your life to shine with a radiant light.

One of the tricks to cultivating mindfulness in the Mindt is to make time each day for yourself. Find a quiet moment where you can retreat to a space of stillness and silence. It can be in the early morning, on a nature walk, or before falling asleep. Choose the time that works best for you and create a personal mindfulness ritual.

During this moment of awareness, bring your attention to your body and your breath. Notice the physical sensations that arise, the movements of your body, the tensions you build up. Embrace these feelings without judgment, letting them dissolve into the flow of the present moment. With your breath, allow calm to envelop you, releasing accumulated worries and tensions.

Another method for developing awareness is the observation of thoughts and emotions. Take note of the thoughts that cross your mind, without identifying with them. Notice how emotions rush into your heart, welcoming them with kindness and acceptance. This act of observation without judgment allows you to develop a deep awareness of your internal experiences, opening spaces for freedom and conscious choice.

Throughout your day, find moments to bring your attention to the present. You can do this through the practice of mindful breathing by focusing on the rhythm of your breath and letting it guide you in the present moment. You can also use reminders, such as a timer or an app on your phone, to remind you to take mindfulness breaks throughout the day. In those moments, take a few moments to observe yourself, to recognize your sensations, thoughts and emotions.

Mindfulness awareness also extends to your relationships with others. When in conversation with someone, practice active listening and full presence. Take note of each other's words, body language, and nuances of emotion. Show genuine interest and genuine attention, creating spaces for connection and deep understanding.

The constant practice of these methods will lead you towards an awareness that is increasingly rooted in your daily life. You will find that mindfulness becomes a natural quality, permeating your actions, thoughts and relationships. Your life will be enriched with moments of presence and joy, while your psychological and physical well-being will strengthen.

Trust Mindt and let mindfulness become a faithful companion on your journey to wellbeing. Be patient with yourself, give yourself the time and space to explore the depths of awareness. Mindt supports you in your search for a conscious and meaningful life, bringing light and serenity along the way.

It is important to practice meditation. Meditation is an effective method for developing mindfulness. You can meditate at any time of the day, even for just a few minutes. Meditation helps you focus on the present and accept feelings and emotions without judgment.
Meditation is a precious gift that you can give yourself every day. It's like a caress for the soul, a moment of deep connection with yourself and with the present. Meditation practice is an opportunity to develop your awareness in a powerful and effective way.

You can find spaces for meditation at any time of the day, even for just a few minutes. It can be a quiet moment in the early morning, a break during lunch or a moment of reflection before falling asleep. Find the moment that works best for you and create a personal meditation ritual.

When you immerse yourself in meditation, let your breath become your guide in the present moment. Allow your attention to focus on the rhythm of your breath, noting how it enters and leaves your body. With each inhalation, let calmness and serenity wash over you. With each exhalation, let go of the tensions and worries that have built up.

Meditation teaches you to welcome sensations and emotions without judgment. As you meditate, you may notice thoughts or emotions arising in your mind. Let them show up as clouds floating across the sky. Observe them without clinging to them or judging them. Accept each sensation and emotion with kindness, letting them flow into the flow of the present moment.

Through constant meditation practice, you develop a deep awareness of yourself and the world around you. You learn to notice details that often escape ordinary attention. Discover the beauty of a blossoming flower, the sound of footsteps on the earth, the feel of the sun on your skin. Meditation allows you to fully immerse yourself in the present, to embrace the essence of life with gratitude and wonder.

Meditation is a path of personal growth and inner transformation. With each breath, you can cultivate inner calm, emotional balance, and a deep connection with your authentic self. Allow yourself this space of peace and silence, allowing meditation to nourish your soul and awaken your deepest awareness.
Trust meditation as a loving guide on your path to mindfulness and well-being. Remember that every moment of meditation is an opportunity to reconnect with yourself and the beauty in life. Let meditation envelop you in its sweetness and reveal new dimensions of peace, joy and awareness. Give yourself the precious gift of meditation, a moment of deep breath and connection with your most authentic essence. It's like diving into an ocean of serenity, letting the waves of your breath gently rock you.
Meditation is a safe haven where you can find inner peace and needed solitude. As you immerse yourself in this state of awareness, let your breath become your anchor to the present moment.

Each inhalation brings you back to life, while each exhalation releases your being from tensions and worries.

In meditation, there is no room for judgment. Welcome every feeling and every emotion with kindness and acceptance. Let the emotions flow through you like a river, without clinging to them or pushing them away. Through this practice of non-judgment, you discover the beauty of your true nature.

Meditation is a silent dance between your body and your mind. Take the time to observe the thoughts that pop into your mind, like clouds passing across the sky. Be a detached observer, not identifying yourself with the thoughts that arise. In this space of awareness, you can discover a freedom that goes beyond the limitations of the mind.

Regular meditation practice is a key to cultivating mindfulness in every aspect of your life. It allows you to be present in the present moment, to tune in to your intuition and to connect with your inner wisdom. You will find that even daily challenges can be faced with serenity and clarity.

Meditation does not require sophisticated equipment or special environments. You can meditate wherever you are, at any time of the day. Just find a quiet place and take a few moments for yourself. It can be a break in the chaos of everyday life or a moment of reflection before starting the day. Choose the moment that resonates with you and allow yourself this wonderful mindfulness experience.

Meditation is a loving embrace for your mind, body and soul. It's a practice that nourishes your most authentic essence, connects you with the vital flow of the universe and allows you to find inner balance again. Rely on meditation as an invaluable guide and let it accompany you every step of the way to self-awareness and self-realization.

Discover the joy of finding yourself in the silence of meditation. Let the breath surround you like a caress, as you immerse your mind in a sea of tranquility. Meditation will reveal deep secrets and hidden treasures to you, bringing light and harmony into your life. Allow yourself this moment of wisdom and serenity, letting meditation guide you to the beauty of your true nature.

Another method to develop awareness is the practice of Mindful Eating. Mindful Eating consists in eating mindfully, paying attention to the flavours, sensations and emotions that one experiences during the meal. This helps develop awareness of your body and your nutritional needs. Immerse yourself in an extraordinary sensory experience through the practice of Mindful Eating, a tasty journey that connects you with your body and your nutritional needs. It's like savoring every bite as if it were a precious gift, embracing every sensation and every emotion that the act of eating offers you.

Mindful Eating invites you to pay attention to the flavors dancing on your tongue. Savor each bite as if it were a work of art, allowing flavors to expand and envelop you in sublime sweetness. Let the food delight you with its unique texture, aroma and flavour. Every bite is an opportunity to discover new shades of pleasure and to connect with the nutritional power of foods.

During the meal, let your awareness extend to the physical sensations arising in your body. Notice feelings of hunger and satiety, lightness or heaviness. Watch how food is digested, how it moves through your digestive system. With mindfulness, you develop an intimate relationship with your body, respecting its needs and nurturing it with love and gratitude.

Mindful Eating also invites you to explore your emotions related to food. See if you feel joy, comfort, stress, or sadness during the meal. Welcome these emotions without judgment, letting them manifest and dissolve. Food becomes a bridge to better understand yourself, to recognize your eating habits and to create a more balanced relationship with food.

This conscious approach to food allows you to make more informed and healthy food choices. You develop a deep intuition about the foods that satisfy your body and truly nourish it. It's not just about nourishing the body, but also about nourishing the soul, choosing foods that give you energy, vitality and well-being.

Mindful Eating is an invitation to slow down and fully enjoy each meal. Abandon the hustle and bustle of daily life, give yourself time to sit back, breathe deeply and appreciate the food in front of you. Stay present in the moment, letting mindfulness guide you through a dining experience that feeds not only your body, but your soul as well.

Trust Mindful Eating as a precious ally on your journey towards a healthy and harmonious relationship with food. Be kind to yourself, letting mindfulness guide your food choices and lead you to lasting well-being. Discover the joy of nourishing your body with love, gratitude and mindful attention. Every meal becomes an opportunity to celebrate life and to feed your soul with every bite. Immerse yourself in a culinary experience that awakens your senses and nourishes your soul. Mindful Eating offers you a journey of discovery and pleasure, where every bite becomes a moment of deep connection with yourself and with the food that nourishes you.

When you practice Mindful Eating, let your senses be guided by curiosity and gratitude. Look at food with new eyes, as if it were a wonder to be discovered. Observe its bright colors, its unique shapes and let yourself be enveloped by the beauty of its details. With your sense of touch, you discover the texture of foods that touch your tongue, feel their consistency and let them fall apart gently in your mouth.

Mindful Eating invites you to pay attention to the flavors that spread on your palate. Savor each bite with gratitude and fullness, noting the nuances of sweetness, acidity, bitterness or savory. Let the food dance on your tongue, unleashing a symphony of sensations that blend harmoniously. Mindfulness allows you to savor each bite as if it were a precious gift.

During your meal, take the time to chew slowly and mindfully. Feel the rhythmic movement of your jaw, the transformation of foods as they are broken into smaller pieces. With each chew, you allow the food to fuse with your saliva, being prepared for digestion. Your awareness extends to the very process of eating, nurturing your body with care and respect.

Mindful Eating also invites you to connect with your emotions related to food. See if you feel joy, sadness, satisfaction, or frustration while eating. Welcome these emotions without judgment, letting them emerge and fade away like waves on the ocean. Find out how food can be an emotional support or an opportunity to explore and better understand your emotions.

Through Mindful Eating, you can create a healthier and more mindful relationship with food. You develop greater awareness of your nutritional needs and learn to listen to your body. Food becomes an ally in your quest for well-being and vitality. Every meal becomes an opportunity to nourish not only your body, but your soul as well.

Trust Mindful Eating as a faithful companion on your path to mindfulness and health. Be present in the moment, letting every bite be an act of self-love. Discover the joy of nourishing your body with attention and gratitude, of creating a harmonious relationship with the food that nourishes you. Mindful Eating invites you to experience a deep connection with food, a dance of awareness and pleasure that enriches every aspect of your life.

Also, it's important to take time for yourself. Daily life can be very hectic and stressful. Taking time for yourself helps you relax and develop awareness of your own needs and limits.

Self-observation is a precious key to unlocking the doors of awareness and inner freedom. It's like lighting the corridors of your mind, exploring your thoughts and emotions without judgment. Through self-observation, you can free yourself from limiting mental patterns and cultivate a more authentic relationship with yourself and with others.

When you practice self-observation, give yourself the gift of being present in the present moment. Be aware of your thoughts, your inner dialogues that unfold like a dance in your mind. Observe these thoughts as a detached spectator, without identifying with them. Notice what your recurring patterns are, what thoughts bring you joy or cause you worries. Awareness allows you to discover the roots of your thoughts, to explore them with curiosity and to consciously choose the ones you need for your well-being.

Self-observation also invites you to pay attention to your emotions, to recognize the nuances and intensities that manifest within you. Welcome every emotion with kindness, without labeling it as good or bad. Observe how emotions manifest in your body, how they move and dissolve in the flow of the present moment. This act of awareness allows you to better understand yourself and navigate wisely through the sea of emotions.

Self-observation is an opportunity to free yourself from the shackles of conditioning and automatic reactions. It invites you to become aware of your behaviors, your emotional reactions and to take command of your life. Through self-observation, you can create spaces of freedom where you can choose how you respond to the challenges and situations you encounter along the way.

This practice connects you to the transformative power of the here and now, where every moment is an opportunity to grow and evolve. Self-observation allows you to free yourself from judgments and expectations, to embrace your authenticity, and to cultivate more authentic relationships with others. With mindfulness, you can create a space of understanding and empathy, welcoming others in their uniqueness.

Rely on self-observation as a valuable guide in your search for freedom and authenticity. Be patient with yourself, take the time to explore the depths of your mind and heart. Self-observation leads you to a deeper awareness of yourself and the world around you. It allows you to cultivate more authentic relationships, make informed decisions, and embrace the fullness of life.

Discover the beauty of being the conscious witness of your existence. Let self-observation lead you to an inner freedom that shines like a bright sun. Through this journey of awareness, you can embrace the fullness of who you truly are and discover the power to create an authentic and meaningful life.

In summary, there are several methods and practical tricks to develop awareness in the Mindt. Meditation, Mindful Eating, taking time for yourself and self-observation are just some of the techniques that can help develop mindfulness. With constant practice, mindfulness will become an integral part of one's life and one will be able to enjoy greater inner peace and a better quality of life. Awareness is a precious gem that can transform your life, and in Mindt you will find a series of practical methods and tricks to cultivate it with passion and dedication. Immerse yourself in an ocean of wisdom and embrace the beauty in your existence through these powerful practices.

Meditation offers you a space of tranquility and intimacy with yourself. Give yourself the gift of sitting in silence, letting your breath guide you into the present moment. Observe your thoughts appearing in your mind like clouds, without holding on to them. Be present and aware of your body, your sensations and your emotions. With consistent practice, meditation will become a beacon of inner peace and a source of inspiration in your life.

Mindful Eating is an invitation to live each meal as a sensory experience. Immerse yourself in the joy of savoring every bite, paying attention to the flavors that dance on your tongue and the sensations that awaken in your body. Take the time to feed yourself with awareness and gratitude, listening to your body's needs and approaching food with love and respect. Through Mindful Eating, you will discover a new level of connection with yourself and with the food that nourishes you.

Take some precious time for yourself, allow yourself moments of sweet solitude and personal care. Be kind to yourself by setting aside spaces in your schedule for nurturing practices, such as reading an inspiring book, taking a walk in nature, or taking up a creative hobby. Give yourself the luxury of slowing down the hectic pace of life and reconnecting with your most authentic essence. In these moments of serenity, mindfulness will strengthen and guide you towards a more balanced and fulfilling life.

Self-observation is an act of self-love. Observe your thoughts, emotions, and reactions without judgment. Be aware of your mental patterns, habits and behaviors. With mindfulness, you can take charge of your life, freeing yourself from automatic reactions and consciously choosing how to respond to the challenges life presents you. Through self-observation, you will develop a radiant authenticity and a deep connection with yourself and with others.

With dedication and consistent practice, mindfulness will take root more and more deeply in your life. You will discover greater inner peace, clarity of mind and a more authentic connection with yourself and with others. Give yourself the gift of developing awareness in the Mindt and enjoy the wonderful fruits it will bring into your life.

Explore the transformative power of mindfulness and embrace the joy of living with an open mind and heart. Mindt gives you practical tools and invaluable tricks for developing mindfulness and living a meaningful life. Be present in the moment, cultivate awareness and embrace the beauty that every moment brings. Your awareness is the key to unlocking the doors of authenticity and lasting happiness.

CHAPTER 9. THE IMPORTANCE OF PRACTICE IN THE MINDT.

Mindfulness Training (Mindt) is a meditation technique that requires constant and regular practice in order to obtain its benefits. In fact, the importance of the practice in the Mindt is essential to achieve greater awareness of oneself and of the surrounding environment.

Mindt's practice is to be present in the present moment, without judging or evaluating what is happening around us. This state of conscious attention allows us to live the present in a more intense and serene way, without losing mental energy in useless and stressful thoughts. In embracing Mindfulness Training (Mindt), immerse yourself in the flow of life with a fiery and passionate awareness. Constant practice is the key that opens the door to inner transformation and a more authentic life.

Mindt invites us to slow down the frenetic pace of life and immerse ourselves in the present, embracing every moment with total presence. It is like a gentle caress that envelops us, allowing us to tune in to the vibrant colors of life and to embrace each experience with gratitude and acceptance.

With constant practice, Mindt helps us free ourselves from the chains of thoughts and worries that imprison us, allowing us to fully enjoy every moment. It offers us a fresh new perspective, an opportunity to live without regrets about the past or anxieties about the future.

Regular Mindt practice connects us with our true essence, makes us rediscover the wonder of the simple act of breathing and teaches us to be compassionate towards ourselves and others. It helps us cultivate a deep connection with our body, our emotions and our thoughts, allowing us to live a more authentic and rewarding life.

Mindt requires discipline and dedication, but its benefits are endless. It allows us to discover the beauty in the little things, to embrace the joy in the present, and to live with radiant awareness. It gives us the freedom to be authentic, to embrace our uniqueness and to live in harmony with the world around us.

Be brave and bet on yourself. Embrace Mindfulness Training as a travel companion, exploring the deep mysteries of your mind and heart. With regular practice, you will discover a new dimension of inner peace, wisdom and gratitude.

Immerse yourself in the beauty of the present moment. Be present with the flowing breath, with the beating of your heart and with the wonders that surround you. Recognize the power of your awareness and let it shine as a radiant light in your life.

Mindt is an invitation to live more fully and authentically. It is a call to awaken your true essence and to live with passion and gratitude. Be brave and embrace regular Mindt practice, discovering the joy of living with radiant awareness and an open heart.

Let Mindfulness Training weave itself into the fabric of your life, transforming the way you see yourself and the world around you. Awareness is the common thread that will guide you towards a more authentic life, full of joy and serenity. Choose to embrace Mindt as a precious gift that will accompany you in every step of your journey towards awareness and inner freedom. Be bold and let Mindfulness Training (Mindt) creep into the fabric of your life, warming your heart and awakening your soul. It's an exciting journey, a dive into the ocean of awareness that will transform you profoundly.

Mindt invites you to immerse yourself in the present with your whole being. Take a break from the hustle and bustle of life and give yourself the luxury of just being. Give yourself permission to let go of the burden of the past and worries about the future. Relax and tune into the present moment, letting awareness spread like a warm, loving embrace.

Regular Mindt practice is like a sacred ritual that connects you with your most authentic essence. Sit quietly and let your attention settle on your breath, feeling the air flowing in and out of your body. Observe the thoughts floating in your mind like clouds in the sky, without holding on to them. Welcome every emotion that arises in your heart with kindness and acceptance. Be present with your body, feeling the sensations that occur in every moment.

The Mindt is a harmonious dance between you and the present moment. It allows you to live every moment with vibrant awareness, savoring every experience as a precious gift. You can feel the breeze on your face, hear the birds singing and smell the flowers with renewed depth and gratitude.

Through Mindt, you will discover the power of mindfulness to transform the way you relate to yourself and others. You will be able to cultivate more authentic communication, respond to challenges with poise, and live with a serenity that emanates from within. Mindfulness allows you to connect with your inner compass, follow your heart, and create a life aligned with your deepest values.

Be brave and immerse yourself in the adventure of Mindfulness Training. Discover the joy of living with an authentic presence, embracing each moment with gratitude and wonder. Watch the change unfold in and around you as your awareness takes root and expands like a tree reaching into the sky.

The Mindt is a journey to self-discovery, to liberation from the shackles of the mind, and to a life lived with an open heart. It is an invitation to live with radiant awareness, to dance with life and to celebrate the beauty of the present. Be bold and embrace Mindfulness Training as a life partner who will accompany you with love and wisdom along your path.

To reap these benefits, you need to take the time to practice Mindt daily. This means that you need to find a time of day when you can sit quietly and focus on your breathing and the sensations in your body.

The constant practice of Mindt allows us to develop greater awareness of ourselves, our emotions and our thoughts. Furthermore, it helps us manage stress and anxiety, improving our ability to concentrate and pay attention. Dedicate a precious moment to your inner growth through the daily practice of Mindfulness Training (Mindt). Find a corner of tranquility, a silent sanctuary where you can immerse yourself in the flow of the present moment. Give yourself the gift of sitting in sweet contemplation, letting your breathing become your connecting link to the here and now.

The constant practice of Mindt is a balm for the soul, an opportunity to slow down the hectic pace of life and to cultivate deep self-awareness. In this sacred space, you can tune in to your emotions, thoughts, and body sensations. Observe them gently and without judgment, welcoming them as treasured guests into the abode of your awareness.

Through regular practice, Mindt will become your traveling companion, illuminating every corner of your existence with a radiant light. You will discover a greater awareness of yourself, your thought patterns and the behavioral patterns that guide you. You will be able to observe your emotions with a loving distance, without being overwhelmed by them. This awareness will give you the freedom to respond to life's challenges with wisdom and compassion.

Mindt is a panacea for the spirit, an anchor of calm in the rough sea of life. Through constant practice, you will be able to face stress and anxiety with a serenity that resides in your heart. You will develop a greater capacity for concentration and attention, allowing you to immerse yourself completely in the present and to fully enjoy the wonders that surround you.

Mindt is not only a solitary practice, it can also be an opportunity to connect with others. You can share your experience with a community of practitioners, creating a deep bond based on mutual awareness and compassion. Together, you can cultivate a collective awareness that permeates every aspect of your life and relationships.

Be brave and give yourself the precious gift of constant practice of Mindfulness Training. Find your rhythm, the time of day that resonates with your soul, and create a sacred space where you can embrace the present with gratitude and openness. With each breath, immerse yourself deeper into awareness, letting your inner light shine with intensity and love.

The Mindt is a journey of discovery and transformation, a journey towards a life lived with an authentic presence and an open heart. Every step you take on the path of awareness brings you closer and closer to your true essence, to the hidden treasures within you. Be true to your practice, be patient with yourself and let Mindfulness Training guide you to a life of serenity, joy and fulfilment. Fully immerse yourself in the transformative power of constant Mindfulness Training (Mindt) practice. Sit in silence, allow your mind to settle, and allow awareness to blossom like a flower in the garden of your being.

Mindt is a balm for the soul, a haven of peace in the chaos of everyday life. Through regular practice, you can sharpen your inward gaze and embrace every aspect of yourself with acceptance and unconditional love. You will discover an oasis of calm within you, a safe haven where you can find rest and healing.

Give yourself the luxury of a moment just for you, where you can let go of your worries and immerse yourself in the flow of the present moment. Your breathing becomes the guiding thread that guides you in the here and now, taking you on a journey of deep awareness. Observe the thoughts floating in your mind like passing clouds, without becoming attached to them. Be kind to yourself, remembering that the mind is like a vast and open sky, where every thought can disappear into thin air and contextually appear there.

Through regular practice of Mindt, you will develop greater awareness of yourself and your automatic reactions. You will be able to recognize mental patterns that limit you and open spaces of freedom within you. Mindfulness allows you to respond wisely to difficult moments instead of reacting impulsively. It helps you cultivate a deep connection with your body, listening to its subtleties and respecting its needs.

Mindt is a beacon of light in the storm, a sure guide in the stormy sea of life. Through constant practice, you will be able to manage stress and anxiety in a more balanced way. Mindfulness allows you to immerse yourself in the present, letting worries about the future dissolve and regrets about the past fade away. With each breath, you find your center again, renewing your inner strength and your ability to face life's challenges with courage.

Mindt is also an invitation to share your experience with others, to create a network of support and connection. Together, you can explore the path of awareness, sharing your challenges, your discoveries and your joys. You will find comfort in collective awareness and mutual support.

Be bold and embrace the power of constant mindfulness training practice. Discover the very essence of life in the present moment, embracing each moment with gratitude and wonder. Let awareness permeate every aspect of your existence, giving you a life lived with intensity and love. With each breath, dive deeper into the depths of your awareness, discovering the infinite beauty that resides within you.

However, Mindt's practice is not always easy and requires commitment and perseverance. It is important not to get discouraged when faced with difficulties and to continue practicing regularly, even when the results are not immediate. On the path of Mindfulness Training (Mindt), we face challenges and obstacles that can test our resolve. But remember, even the greatest efforts can lead to wonderful results. Never lose sight of the potential that lies within you and keep the flame of your practice alive.

Yes, there will be times when the mind wanders, when distractions take its toll, and when it seems hard to find inner calm. But don't be discouraged, because the true beauty of Mindt lies precisely in perseverance and resilience. Every breath that gently brings you back to awareness, every return to the present is a step towards a richer and more meaningful life.

Be brave and continue to take the time to practice daily, even when it seems like the results aren't immediate. Constancy and commitment will lead you to discover a new world in and around you. Your awareness will deepen, your thoughts will calm down and your heart will open to a dimension of peace and serenity.

Mindt is a journey that requires trust and perseverance. Every conscious breath, every moment of presence becomes a precious piece in the mosaic of your life. Don't worry about how long it will take, but embrace the journey itself as an opportunity for growth and transformation.

Remember that Mindt is not just a set of techniques, but a living experience that takes place in the present moment. Through constant practice, you will discover a greater awareness of yourself, your emotions and your thoughts. You will see that your relationship with the surrounding world will be enriched with depth and understanding.

Don't let challenges get in your way, but let them motivate you to persevere. Every moment of awareness is a step towards a fuller and more authentic life. With each breath, remind yourself of your commitment to yourself and let Mindt be a loving guide on your journey of growth and transformation.

Be brave and continue to practice Mindfulness Training with commitment and perseverance. You will find that your psychological well-being will deepen, your ability to cope with stress will increase, and your quality of life will transform into a fuller and more rewarding experience.

Let your practice be a bright beacon that lights your way, a source of inspiration and guidance along the road to mindfulness. Don't stop dreaming, growing and transforming yourself. With every breath, welcome the gifts Mindfulness Training offers you and enjoy a life lived in radiant awareness.

In conclusion, the importance of the practice in Mindt is fundamental to obtain its benefits. Constancy and commitment in daily practice allow us to develop greater awareness of ourselves and of the surrounding environment, improving our quality of life and our psychological well-being. Be determined and don't let anything distract you from your commitment to constant Mindfulness Training (Mindt) practice. Even when the challenges seem insurmountable and the road seems steep, remember that you have the strength within you to overcome any obstacle.

Mindt is not just a technique, but a lifestyle that embraces awareness and presence in the present moment. It's a path of personal growth, a journey that will lead you to discover the hidden treasures within you. Don't hesitate to embrace the practice wholeheartedly, with confidence and passion.

You will witness wonderful changes manifesting in your life. Mindfulness infiltrates the details, allows you to capture the beauty of small moments, to connect with others on a deeper level. You will discover greater gratitude for the simple things, for the gift of life itself.

Constantly practicing Mindt will give you a new perspective on life. Obstacles will become opportunities for growth, challenges will become milestones on your journey. Each step forward in your practice will lead you towards greater awareness of yourself, your emotions and your reactions.

Don't let distractions divert your attention. Make time each day to sit in silence, to listen to your heartbeat, to merge with the breath flowing through you. Let your practice be a refuge, a moment of refreshment for your mind and spirit.

Be kind to yourself as you practice Mindt. Welcome every moment with patience and without judgment. Remember that the practice is not about perfection, but about the constant effort to cultivate mindfulness. Every breath that is dedicated to your practice is a gift you give yourself, a testament to your love for yourself and for a life lived with presence and gratitude.

Be bold and stick to your commitment. Never stop practicing, even when life's commitments seem to overwhelm you. Mindfulness Training is a bright beacon that shines in your existence, a precious resource that supports you in moments of joy and difficulty.

Remember that your personal practice will positively influence the world around you. Through your awareness, you will be able to spread love, kindness and compassion into your relationships, creating a cascading effect of well-being and harmony.

Be the guardian of your path of awareness and allow Mindt to flourish in your life. Each conscious breath is a step towards a more meaningful life, a testament to your dedication to yourself and your inner growth.

Be proud of your commitment and willingness to cultivate mindfulness in your life. Mindfulness Training is a precious gift that will support you along your journey. With each breath, embrace the beauty and depth of awareness and discover a new dimension of joy and serenity in your life.

CHAPTER 10. HOW TO USE THE MINDT TO IMPROVE INTERPERSONAL RELATIONSHIPS

The Mindt, acronym of "Integrated Method of Negotiation and Treatment of Conflicts", is a methodology that can be used to improve interpersonal relationships in a comprehensive way. This method involves using effective communication techniques, such as active listening and empathy, to understand the other person's needs and find shared solutions to problems. Furthermore, Mindt is based on the creation of a climate of mutual trust and on the valorisation of differences between people, in order to favor cooperation and collaboration.

Thanks to its flexibility and its ability to adapt to different situations, the Mindt can be used in many contexts, such as family, work, school and in general in all those contexts in which interpersonal relationships are important. In conclusion, Mindt represents a valuable tool for improving interpersonal relationships, promoting mutual understanding and collaboration, and allowing conflicts to be faced in a constructive and positive way.

Enter a world of harmony and understanding with Mindt's Integrated Method of Negotiation and Conflict Management. This methodology is the key to building solid and fulfilling interpersonal relationships in every aspect of your life.

Imagine that you are in a conflict situation with a work colleague. Mindt offers you powerful tools to overcome this challenge. Using active listening, you will be able to fully understand the other person's concerns and needs, putting yourself in their perspective.

This authentic form of listening creates fertile ground for mutual understanding and empathy, paving the way for building shared solutions and eliminating barriers that can hinder communication.

Mindt invites you to recognize and value the differences between people. Each individual has a unique set of experiences, values and points of view. Instead of seeing them as obstacles, Mindt encourages you to view these differences as valuable resources that can enrich relationships and spark creativity. By respecting differences, you can create an environment of mutual trust, where every voice is heard and valued.

Mindt is not limited to just resolving conflicts, but aims to promote cooperation and collaboration. Imagine a work team where each member is aware of their strengths and areas for improvement. With Mindt, you'll be able to create an environment where everyone feels an integral part of the decision-making process, where you work together to achieve common goals. This collaborative spirit will lead to amazing results, where the whole exceeds the sum of the parts.

Mindt's flexibility makes it adaptable to different situations and contexts. You can apply it in your family, where there might be a disagreement between members about planning a vacation. With the use of effective communication techniques, you can create an open and respectful dialogue, looking for a solution that takes into account the needs and wishes of each family member. Mindt can also be used in schools, where teachers can foster cooperation and understanding among students, creating an atmosphere of respect and collaboration.

In summary, the Mindt is a treasure to discover to improve your interpersonal relationships. By practicing effective communication techniques, such as active listening and empathy, you can open doors to mutual understanding and cooperation. By valuing the differences between people and creating a climate of trust, you will be able to build solid and authentic bonds.
Mindt is a valuable resource that will guide you in constructive conflict management, paving the way for a world of harmony and collaboration. Immerse yourself in the transformative power of Mindt and discover how interpersonal relationships can become a flourishing garden of love, understanding and collaboration.

Imagine that you are faced with a conflict with a close friend. Mindt offers you a safe space to explore the nuances of conflict, to understand conflicting perspectives, and to seek a solution that respects both sides. Through empathetic listening and being open to dialogue, you can create a bridge of connection and healing that strengthens the bond between the two of you.

Mindt challenges you to go beyond appearances, to go beyond superficial differences. It invites you to dig deeper, to discover what brings people together rather than what divides them. When you embrace diversity and view it as an opportunity to learn and grow, you build bridges of understanding and create spaces where relationships can flourish.

Mindt is distinguished by its collaborative approach, where the common goal becomes more important than individual positions. Imagine you are in a business meeting where different ideas and opinions collide. With Mindt, you can facilitate a negotiation process that considers all perspectives and seeks a solution that benefits all team members. This climate of collaboration stimulates creativity, innovation and the construction of sustainable solutions.

Mindt extends beyond the confines of work and applies to multiple contexts. You can use it in your family circle, where there may be disagreement on decisions regarding child education or financial management. With Mindt's help, you can create spaces for respectful dialogue, where every member of the family feels valued and heard. Together, you can find common ground where you can grow and thrive as a united family.

The Mindt is a beacon of hope and healing for interpersonal relationships. Through its constant practice and commitment, you will be able to cultivate relationships based on trust, understanding and mutual respect. There is no single answer or single way to practice Mindt, but there are endless possibilities for growth and transformation in your relationships.

Be brave and embrace the power of Mindt. With each step forward on your path of interpersonal awareness, you will discover a new dimension of love, connection and harmony. Let Mindt be the key to unlocking the doors to deep and meaningful relationships, where everyone can express themselves authentically and feel truly heard.

Remember that Mindt is a journey that requires commitment and perseverance. There will be moments of challenge and growth, but also moments of joy and gratitude. Through your continued practice, you will witness the beauty and power of interpersonal relationships enriched by mindfulness.

Mindt is your faithful companion along the path of interpersonal relationships. Make it an integral part of your life and you will discover a new way to connect with yourself and with others. Embrace the gift of Mindt and live a life filled with genuine relationships, lovingness and mutual understanding.

Conclusions.

Mindt, with its solid theoretical and multidisciplinary foundation, represents an extraordinary resource for personal growth and relationship management. The integration of principles of psychology, neuroscience and effective communication gives this methodology unprecedented power and depth.
Through Mindt, we are able to better understand the functioning of our mind and our emotional system. This awareness allows us to identify limiting thought patterns and behaviors that can hinder us in achieving our goals. With this knowledge, we can actively work to modify and improve those models, opening up new perspectives and possibilities.
Neuroscience provides a solid scientific basis for understanding how Mindt can affect our mind and body. Studies have shown that constant Mindt practice can lead to positive changes in our brain, improving our ability to focus, manage stress, and regulate emotions. This knowledge offers us a fascinating perspective on the plasticity of the brain and its potential for adaptation and growth.
Effective communication is a fundamental pillar of Mindt. Through active listening, empathy, and the use of assertive communication techniques, Mindt teaches us how to make authentic and meaningful connections with others. We can learn to communicate clearly and empathetically, building trust and mutual respect in our daily interactions.
Mindt intervenes on several levels, acting both on a cognitive and emotional level. Through the practice of mindfulness and being present in the present moment, we can experience increased mental clarity, improved ability to focus, and reduced stress. At the same time, Mindt invites us to connect with our emotions, to recognize them and manage them in a healthy and constructive way.

In conclusion, the Mindt methodology represents an extraordinary opportunity for personal growth and relationship management. Thanks to its solid and multidisciplinary theoretical foundation, it combines elements of psychology, neuroscience and effective communication. Through consistent Mindt practice, we can experience positive changes in our mind, body, and relationships. Be open and ready to embrace this innovative methodology and discover all the potential it can offer in your life. Mindt is more than just a methodology, it's an invitation to explore the boundaries of your mind and heart. It is an exciting and transformative journey, which leads you to discover new depths within yourself and to connect with others in an authentic and profound way.

Through Mindt, you will discover the magic of awareness, the beauty of living in the present moment without judgement. Thoughts become just cloudy passages in the vastness of your being as you immerse yourself in the experience of the here and now. Mindt teaches you to embrace every moment with gratitude, to savor every breath as a precious gift.

At the heart of Mindt is trust in your ability to grow and transform. It challenges you to let go of old mental habits that limit your potential and to experience new perspectives, new ways of thinking and living. You will be surprised at how much you are able to achieve when you open your mind and heart to the possibility of change.

Mindt invites you to dance with your emotions, to explore the depths of your being. She doesn't ask you to suppress or deny your emotions, but to welcome them with kindness and compassion. You will learn to listen to the language of your heart and understand the hidden message behind every emotion. Emotions will become your precious guides, leading you towards your authenticity and your true essence.

Mindt is a light that shines in the dark of conflicts and relationship difficulties. It teaches you to see beyond the surface of people, to recognize their humanity and to cultivate mutual understanding. You'll discover the power of kindness and empathy in building bridges of connection, opening spaces for dialogue, and building meaningful relationships.

Don't worry if the path may seem difficult at times. Mindt will support you along the way, offering tools and practices that will help you overcome obstacles and grow as an individual. You will have the opportunity to meet other people who share your quest for authenticity and connection, creating a community of mutual support and inspiration.

There isn't just one way to practice Mindt, but there are countless paths you can take. Find what resonates with you, what makes you feel alive and full of joy. Mindt is an invitation to discover and celebrate your uniqueness, to live your life in full awareness and with an open heart.

Be bold and embrace the wonder of Mindt. Let me take you on a journey of self discovery and deep connection. The Mindt is a key that opens the door to a more authentic, more meaningful and loving life. Make it part of your journey and let yourself be carried away by the beauty of this unique experience.

Secondly, it should be emphasized that Mindt is a highly personalized method, which takes into account the specific needs and characteristics of each individual. This means that there is no universal solution for everyone, but that each person is addressed in a unique and personalized way.

Furthermore, Mindt is a highly pragmatic approach, focusing on the end goal and the concrete actions needed to achieve it. This means that it is not limited to providing theoretical tools, but focuses above all on the practical implementation of the identified strategies.

Finally, it should be emphasized that Mindt is a highly effective method, which has been shown to achieve concrete results in many areas. Thanks to its flexibility and its ability to customize, Mindt can be used successfully in many contexts, from training to personnel management, from personal development to business consultancy.

In conclusion, Mindt represents an innovative and highly effective approach to improve the quality of life and achieve one's personal and professional goals. In conclusion, Mindt is much more than a

simple methodology, it is an authentic path of transformation and personal growth. Thanks to its solid theoretical basis and its practical effectiveness, it represents a winning choice for those who wish to improve the quality of their life and achieve the desired success.
Mindt offers a personalized approach that adapts to the needs and peculiarities of each individual. It is not a pre-packaged solution, but a path that is built on the basis of your experiences, your goals and your personal challenges. This tailor-made approach allows you to achieve tangible and lasting results, as it takes into account your uniqueness and your specific needs.

What makes Mindt so effective is her ability to integrate knowledge and practices from different disciplines, such as psychology, neuroscience and effective communication. This synergy of approaches allows you to act on multiple levels, working on both the cognitive and emotional spheres. In this way, you can achieve a real inner transformation, which is reflected in your psychological well-being, your productivity and your success.

Mindt offers you concrete tools and practices that you can apply in your daily life. It's not just theory, but proven methods that help you deal with challenges, manage stress, improve your ability to focus, and develop more meaningful interpersonal relationships. You can apply Mindt in different areas of your life, whether it's work, family, studies or any other context in which you want to improve your performance and achieve your goals.

Mindt is an invitation to take charge of your life and become the protagonist of your success. Through constant effort and regular practice, you can experience the benefits of this innovative approach. You will have the opportunity to discover your true potential, to overcome the limitations that held you back in the past, and to embrace a life full of meaning, fulfillment and fulfilment.

Be brave and embrace Mindt as a valuable ally on your journey of personal growth. Choose to invest in yourself and achieve your goals successfully. Mindt is here to guide, support and inspire you along the way. Take control of your life and discover the limitless potential that lies within you. The success you desire is within reach with Mindt. Thanks to its theoretical solidity, its personalization and its practical effectiveness, this method represents a winning choice for anyone wishing to improve their performance and achieve the desired success. Grasp the power of the Mindt tightly and let it transform you into an extraordinary being. Mindt is a road to realizing your dreams, goals and full potential.

Mindt offers you the opportunity to challenge your limiting beliefs and embrace new perspectives. You can overcome the obstacles that stand in your way and embrace the success you deserve. This method teaches you to create a harmonious balance between your mind, body and spirit, enabling you to live a full and fulfilling life.
Whether you're looking to achieve professional success, improve your relationships, or find a sense of inner peace and contentment, Mindt is your trusted ally.
It will guide you step by step, providing you with the tools and practices you need to turn your dreams into reality.

Mindt is a light that shines in the dark, a beacon of hope and change. No matter what challenges you face, Mindt will support you in your growth journey and help you overcome any obstacles. You'll have the ability to discover internal resources you didn't even know you possessed, unleashing your unlimited potential.

Take courage into your own hands and embrace the transformative power of Mindt. Choose to invest in yourself and create the life you truly desire. Mindt offers you a gateway to success, happiness and personal fulfillment.

Don't allow your fears or doubts to hold you back. Mindt is here for you, ready to accompany you on your journey of growth and change. With her support, you can become the best version of yourself, living a life full of joy, discovery and meaning.

Don't wait any longer. Take the first step towards your transformation with Mindt. Trust this extraordinary methodology and discover the power that resides within you. Your life can become a masterpiece, a testament to your courage and willingness to pursue success and happiness.

Mindt invites you to embrace change and dance to the rhythm of your own essence. Be bold, be authentic, and discover the beauty of a life lived with awareness and intention. Mindt is your travel companion, ready to support, inspire and guide you along the path to success and fulfilment. Take your life into your own hands and embrace the wonder of Mindt.

Appendix.

Here are some practical examples of how the Mindt method can be applied to address different issues:

1. Problem: Performance anxiety in the workplace

- Without Mindt method: The person experiences severe anxiety before presentations or meetings, compromising their performance and self-confidence.

- With the Mindt method: Through awareness and conscious breathing, the person learns to manage anxiety and to remain calm during stressful work situations, allowing for greater safety and concentration.

2. Problem: Difficulty managing emotions

- Without Mindt method: The person feels overwhelmed by their emotions, reacting impulsively and damaging interpersonal relationships.

- With Mindt method: Through self-observation and acceptance of emotions, the person learns to manage their emotions in a healthy and constructive way, improving the quality of interactions and favoring greater emotional stability.

3. Problem: Difficulty concentrating and paying attention

- Without Mindt method: The person feels easily distracted and struggles to maintain focus on a task, compromising productivity and efficiency.

- With Mindt method: Through the practice of awareness and attention to the present moment, the person develops greater concentration and attention, increasing their productivity and achieving higher quality results.

4. Problem: Difficulty managing stress

- Without Mindt method: The person feels overwhelmed by daily stress, experiencing anxiety, muscle tension and fatigue.

- With Mindt method: Through the regular practice of Mindt, the person develops greater awareness of stressful stimuli and learns relaxation techniques such as deep breathing and visualization, reducing stress and promoting greater inner calm.

5. Problem: Communication difficulties in personal relationships

- Without Mindt method: The person experiences conflicts and misunderstandings in relationships, due to unclear or aggressive communication.

- With the Mindt method: Through the application of effective communication techniques such as active listening and empathy, the person develops a more open and respectful communication, facilitating conflict resolution and improving the quality of relationships.

Here are other practical examples of how the Mindt method can be applied to address different issues:

6. Problem: Difficulty making important decisions
- Without Mindt method: The person feels confused and indecisive in the face of crucial choices, postponing decisions and generating anxiety.
- With Mindt method: Using the awareness of the present moment, the person learns to connect with their intuition and to make informed decisions, based on inner wisdom and on understanding their own needs and values.

7. Problem: Difficulty managing time and priorities
- Without Mindt method: The person feels overwhelmed by the numerous responsibilities and tasks to be carried out, wasting energy on non-priority activities.
- With Mindt method: Through awareness of the present moment and focus on the priority of events, the person learns to manage time effectively, focusing their energies on the most important activities and creating a space for rest and recovery.

8. Problem: Difficulty managing interpersonal conflicts
- Without Mindt method: The person feels involved in recurring conflicts, reacting impulsively and amplifying tensions.
- With the Mindt method: Through the application of negotiation and active listening techniques, the person develops greater awareness of their own emotional reactions and learns to manage conflicts constructively, promoting mutual understanding and the search for shared solutions.

9. Problem: Difficulty managing negative emotions
- Without Mindt method: The person feels overwhelmed by emotions such as anger, sadness or fear, reacting impulsively and damaging relationships.
- With Mindt method: Through self-observation and acceptance of negative emotions, the person learns to manage and regulate their emotions, developing greater emotional stability and fostering more harmonious and satisfying relationships.
10. Problem: Difficulty managing burnout* and feeling overwhelmed
- Without Mindt method: The person feels exhausted and overwhelmed by work or personal demands, experiencing a sense of distrust and loss of motivation.
- With the Mindt method: Through the practice of awareness and self-care, the person learns to take care of themselves, to recognize their limits and to create balance in their lives, preventing burnout and recovering a sense of confidence and vitality .

These examples demonstrate how Mindt can be an invaluable tool in addressing a wide range of personal and professional issues. Its flexibility and adaptability make it a powerful resource for promoting well-being and success in every aspect of life. Experience Mindt and discover how this innovative methodology can transform your life in surprising and meaningful ways. These are just a few examples of how Mindt can be applied to address different issues. Everyone has their own unique challenges and needs, and the Mindt Method can be individually tailored to meet individual needs. By experimenting with Mindt, you will discover how this innovative approach can bring tangible and significant benefits to your life.

*As WHO (World Health Organization) suggests, burnout is a state of chronic work-related stress characterized by the feeling of complete exhaustion of one's physical and mental energies.

Notes and references on Mindt.

Mindt is a language analysis methodology that focuses on identifying micro-patterns within a text. This technique was developed by Michael Mindt, a German linguist and university professor, and is based on the use of IT tools for text analysis.

Mindt has been successfully applied in various fields, from linguistics to psychology, from literature to corporate communication. Thanks to its ability to identify the most subtle details of a text, Mindt can be used to improve understanding of the messages communicated and to optimize communication itself.

In particular, Mindt focuses on the analysis of so-called "colocations", or words that tend to appear together in a text. These collocations can be used to identify the main themes of the text and to spot any ambiguities or contradictions.

The Mindt can be used both for the analysis of written texts and for the analysis of spoken discourses. In both cases, the technique is based on the use of specific software which makes it possible to identify the most frequent locations and analyze them in detail.

As already mentioned, when it comes to analyzing written texts or spoken speech, Mindt offers a wide range of specific software that will help you explore the most frequent locations in detail. These advanced tools are designed to allow you to uncover the subtle connections between words, revealing hidden meanings and patterns that might otherwise be overlooked.

One of the flagship software offered by Mindt is the powerful "Mindt Analyzer". This smart tool allows you to easily upload your written texts or speeches and get a complete overview of the most relevant collocations. The Mindt Analyzer uses sophisticated natural language processing algorithms to identify and analyze the relationships between words, helping you discover new levels of meaning and depth in your texts.

In addition, Mindt also offers you the "Collocation Explorer" software. This tool allows you to explore collocations in an interactive and intuitive way. With a user-friendly interface, the Collocation Explorer allows you to view collocations in a graphical format, highlighting keywords and their connections. You can explore locations dynamically, zooming in or out to uncover hidden details and meaningful relationships.

For more experienced analysts, Mindt also offers the "Collocation Profiler" software. This advanced tool allows you to conduct detailed analysis on placements, providing a wide range of statistics and graphs for in-depth analysis. You can explore word frequencies, co-occurrence, usage contexts and much more, giving you a complete overview of the linguistic relationships present in your texts or speeches.

Whether you're a writer, speaker, or researcher, these software tools from Mindt will provide you with unique insight into the locations in your language material. You'll discover new meanings, find hidden patterns, and increase your understanding of language so you can communicate with even greater precision and clarity.

Don't miss the opportunity to explore the universe of collocations and deepen your understanding of language. Take advantage of the software offered by Mindt and discover the unlimited potential of your words. The world of linguistic analysis is at your fingertips.

In conclusion, the Mindt represents an extremely useful tool for language analysis and can be used in different contexts. Thanks to its ability to identify the most subtle details of a text, Mindt allows you to improve the understanding of the messages communicated and to optimize the communication itself.

In conclusion, Mindt represents a powerful tool for language analysis that opens new horizons in understanding and communication. Thanks to her ability to scrutinize the subtlest details of a text, Mindt invites us to immerse ourselves in a world of hidden meanings and linguistic nuances, revealing the riches that lie behind the words.

Through the application of Mindt, we can explore the depths of written texts, analyzing the structures, the semantic connections and the linguistic expressions used. This meticulous analysis allows us to gain a deeper understanding of the messages communicated, capturing every subtle nuance and intention.

The Mindt is particularly useful in contexts such as the analysis of literary texts, academic research, translation and interpretation, but its applications go far beyond that. It can be used for the analysis of political speeches, advertisements, legal texts and in all those contexts in which understanding the language is essential.

With Mindt, we can reveal the implicit meanings and emotions behind words. We can grasp the cultural and historical aspects that permeate a text, better understanding the context and the author's intent. Mindt helps us decode language and build bridges of understanding between people, overcoming communication barriers and promoting the sharing of profound meanings.

Its practical application offers us a unique opportunity to discover the infinite nuances of human language and to reveal the hidden potential of the texts that surround us. Mindt invites us to go beyond words, to immerse ourselves in the fascinating universe of linguistic expressions and to grasp the very essence of communication.

In conclusion, Mindt is a powerful tool that opens the door to a world of deep understanding and effective communication. With her guidance, we can explore language with fresh eyes, hone our interpretive skills, and uncover the beauty and complexity behind every word. Let us be conquered by the wonder of Mindt and discover the infinite possibilities it offers us in the exploration of human language. In this adventure into Mindt's world, we come across a transformative power that is beyond words. Mindt invites us on a journey of self exploration and deep connection with the language that surrounds us.

Through the Mindt, we can discover the emotions that hide behind every written or spoken word. We can catch the nuances of love, joy, pain and hope that weave between the lines of a poem, a novel or an impassioned speech.

Mindt pushes us to look beyond appearances, to penetrate the soul of words to discover their most authentic essence. We can sense the challenges and desires behind every request, every nonverbal communication, and every meaningful silence.

Through Mindt, we learn to be present, to fully immerse ourselves in the present moment and to grasp every detail that enriches our relationship with language. We discover the magic of a smile hidden between the lines of a letter, the comfort of a kind word in a time of difficulty and the strength of a promise kept.

Mindt invites us to experience the power of active listening, empathy and deep understanding. We can perceive each other's vibrations, grasp their emotions and build bridges of connection that go beyond the words themselves.

At the heart of Mindt we find a beautiful dance between the intellect and the heart, a symphony of meanings that blend and enrich each other. Thanks to this dance, we can express our most authentic truth and understand each other in a deep and intimate way.

The Mindt is a tool of discovery, connection and elevation of human language. It challenges us to explore the boundaries of our understanding and to overcome the barriers that separate us. It invites us to recognize the beauty and power of words, to use them wisely and to cultivate a respectful and authentic dialogue.

On this journey of discovery with Mindt, we open the door to a new way to communicate, understand and connect. We are ready to embrace the richness and depth of human language, letting ourselves be moved and transformed by its infinite nuances.

Discover the magic of Mindt, embrace the beauty of language and unleash your communication potential. Through Mindt, the world of words reveals itself as a treasure to be explored, an infinite universe of emotions and connections that enrich our life experience.

END.